Lose My Location

Freshwater

Freshwater Press

United States of America

All Scripture references are from the KJV unless otherwise indicated.

Freshwater Press, United States of America

ISBN: 978-1-960150-01-1

Printed in the U.S.A.

CONTENTS

A shout out to Dr. Daniel Olukoya (*Freedom from Human Persecutors*, *Prayer Rain*) and Dr. Daniel Duval (*Evil Human Persecutors Prayer*), both whose ministries I sit under, whose teachings I admire, and whose prayer points are a dynamic blessing in my life.

Prologue

A woman wanted to take up jogging, but she said it scared her too much. Every time she'd run, she felt like there was someone following her, so she'd stop and turn around. Every time she turned around there was no one following her. She then soon realized that no one was back there, she just had too much junk in the trunk.

LOL.

Ha-ha.

Very funny.

Too Much Junk in the Trunk

Meanwhile, in real life, have you ever noticed that that almost everywhere you go, there is someone that you know? While out and about, do you bump into people that you've had relationships, connections with, that you're really not expecting to see--, but there they are? You go on vacation halfway, or all the way around the world, and you run into someone from your *hometown*. It's a little confusing; how does this even happen?

You're at Disney Land, hanging out with Mickey and what do you know, there's your 2nd cousin that you haven't seen in 12 years, who lives even further away from Disney Land than you do. He's right where you are, at the exact same time that you're there, that's wild, *isn't it?*

You get a job and there's someone from your high school already working there – and not a favorite person at all. If you had known he or she was there, you might have not applied. Or maybe you do get the job, and a week later, your grade school bully applies at the same place. Man! This is a job that you really wanted; so, you're going to stick it out.

Maybe this is the Lord's way of making us reconcile with others, not leaving things undone. Perhaps it's God's way of making us reconcile with our past. I heard someone say once that the more God loves you, the less He lets you get away with. Saints of God, if this is God's way, God's plan, that we stay reconciled with others, we obey God, because this is love.

Encountering people from yesteryear might just be a nice coincidence, but do coincidences *keep* happening? A nice coincidence? How come its always people that you don't care for, or don't like. Not your favorite people.

Have you ever asked yourself, *why*? Why these people? Why here, at a job that you must come to 5 days a week? It's like being in school all over again. Why the nosy people? Why the busy bodies? It would be so much better to run into or work with some people that you really like.

But we should just live and let live – nope, not these people. Why are they *all up* in your business? Why don't they mind their own business?

Unfriendly Friends

Haters--, *all up* in your grill, your Kool-Aid, your business, your life. You're not even real friends with them. Associates? No, they call themselves your friends, but you know them as **unfriendly** friends, people who are trying to find out what you're doing, who are you with, where's your house and what is it like? Friends with *comparison-itis*. You can do without that, right?

Ones who call you to tell you that the Lord has a 'word' for you, when you don't even know what *lord* they are talking to, and who they are talking about, because you know how they live. You know their lifestyle. They are really just digging into your business. That so called *'word' ain't got nothing to do with you.* Actually, they are asking you more questions than giving you answers because there is no 'word,' they are just digging. They are prying into your business, and into your life. Who needs that?

It's not as though you're doing something crooked, secret or trying to hide a crime, a sin, or anything, you're just living your life. But it seems like there's some nosy little bird, as it were there to report it. To whom?

Maybe they report it to anyone who will listen--, or worse.

You're a private person. Else, you, yourself would plaster your own life on Facebook, Insta or some other social media platform. Maybe that's the problem. You're **not** putting your business out in the streets, out on social media, so a lot of people may be wanting to know what you're doing, how you're doing and how you're doing *it*. They are not all good – I mean, some are.

Discern every *spirit*.

Don't Let Them Know

the Length of You

Perhaps there are times you may have **bragged,** and you shouldn't have. It's not always wise to put all your business on blast, no matter how happy you are about your current circumstances.

In the Bible:

> Hezekiah received the envoys and showed them all that was in his storehouses—the silver, the gold, the spices and the fine olive oil—his armory and everything found among his treasures. There was nothing in

his palace or in all his kingdom that
Hezekiah did not show them.

(2 Kings 20:13 NIV)

King Hezekiah, a natural man,
was showing his kingdom, armory, and
treasury off, as a carnal, natural man is
known to do. Next thing you know he's
being attacked and robbed. Those who
came to see the kingdom were *casing
the joint.*

You're a *little king* in the Earth.
Don't put all your business on Social
Media. Don't tell of all your silver and
gold and precious belongings. Don't put
all your fine things out there. My daddy
said, *"Don't let them know the length of*

you." Don't tell all of your business like that.

Further, in that chapter of the Bible, Isaiah wanted to know of King Hezekiah, *"Who are these men and what did you show them?"*

King Hezekiah answered, *"They were from a very far away land, and I showed them everything."*

The word then was pronounced by the prophet, Isaiah, "You're going to go into captivity," – and we can surmise, because he put all of his riches and stuff, **out there.**

Conversely, King Solomon was the richest of all kings – ever. Hc entertained people who were amazed and astonished by how he *put on the dog*. His palace, hospitality, and kingdom took their breath away. Yet, King Solomon was so wise and had sought God prior, so nobody tried to rob Solomon.

Social media is not there for you to show the world, all your friends, so-called friends, haters, and enemies **everything**. UNLESS GOD told you to show off *everything* that He's given you. If you're making your boast in the LORD, that is another thing, entirely. Most who are showing off all their "stuff", are saying, *"Look at ME, look at what I did. Look at what I did all by myself."*

Your life can be an open book to God, and to the Spirit of God who is leading you into all truth, into knowledge, wisdom, understanding, guiding you, for the sake of the Gospel into your purpose, ministry, life, godliness, and destiny. New house? New car? New clothes? Vacation? Sure, share and have some fun with it. Share with the people you know and trust. Select your audience. Telling all your business to the whole world is not wise. Be sure to make your boast in the Lord. Make your boast God-focused. Bless the Lord. Look at what the Lord has done for me.

My soul shall make her boast in the LORD: the humble shall hear *thereof,*

and be glad. (Psalm 34:2)

Thinking of You

I think everybody has or has had at least one **unfriendly friend.** Until you learn better, you may think that you can share your goals, plans, successes, and achievements with one of these friend-look-alikes. **Unfriendly** friends don't love that you have *anything*, especially not a _new_ something. Not a new house, car, clothes, hat, wig, new dog, and especially not a new relationship. It doesn't matter, there are jealous, covetous-type people everywhere. I'm not saying that everyone is, I am saying that there is an abundance of envious people who are not necessarily going to be happy that you are doing well. Keep discerning.

These people <u>might even be evil, willfully evil</u>. There may come a time that you'd wish they'd *lose your location*. Especially when you are on vacay, wanting to enjoy yourself and relax.

Have you ever been on a cruise, for example, and the people who sit at your dinner table latch on to you and become your *best friends* the whole week, and do everything you do, the entire cruise, then you NEVER hear from them again? Fake friends who didn't have a clue what to do on vacation, so they piggy-backed on your itinerary.

Don't stop discerning.

This book is really about people you do or have known: Unfriendly friends. Fake friends. Evil friends. Former friends. Ex-friends. Ex-boyfriends. Ex-girlfriends. Ex-*in-laws*. You don't hate them; you're Christian, *right?* You've forgiven them how the relationship or situation was, and even how it broke up. But *they're* still holding on to **bitterness** and unforgiveness. And they may even be conjuring up evil against you. Discern every spirit. Be prayerful. Pray without ceasing.

Maybe these people who are doing negative things against you, may not even *realize* they are doing it. Maybe they think *ill* of you. Maybe they think ill of you often, maybe several times a day. Those ill, evil, negative thoughts are the makings of evil arrows. (So, make sure you're not doing that to anyone.)

And when they are thinking these bad thoughts, maybe they, themselves **feel** the feelings they felt when you all parted company and they are reminded of how **bad** it felt. It's a horrible feeling and it may cause them to feel even more negatively about you.

This barrage of strong negative feelings could put them in **survival mode**, which further compounds the problem. A person doesn't know they are not going through the emotional assault that they've conjured up at that very minute, but it _**feels**_ as if they are. Some may panic, some may become anxious and that can all lead to feelings of being in Survival Mode. That mode unleashes a downward spiral of negativity in a person, and if they are emotionally overwhelmed by what they are feeling, they may begin to blame it on **you** instead of understanding that this is a natural response in their _own_ body to acute or chronic negative stimuli—that they are constantly thinking on. It feels horrible. They should also realize that you may not be *doing* anything to them right now, it is them, they are rehearsing all that hurt and pain over and over.

The mind is strong. The mind can respond to evil or good in a tremendous and dramatic way. The mind can make the body think nearly anything, feel, or imagine almost anything.

I notice people in the dental chair on edge, waiting, expecting to feel something, and that something is usually pain. Their teeth could be number than a doorknob, but if they imagine hard enough, they will *believe* they feel something. The hallmark is when they thought they felt something and say, *"Do it again."*

Oh, please. Who is going to ask to feel, or *almost* feel pain, *again?*

The mind is powerful.Either to the positive or the negative, the mind can make a man's life soar to amazing heights or bring the body to its knees.

Its why the Good Book tells us to cast down imaginations.

Casting down imaginations, and every high thing that exalteth itself against the knowledge of God and bringing into captivity every thought to the obedience of Christ; (2 Cor 10:5).

Worse, a person could blindly, in their heart be sending evil to you.

Worst, they **are** evil and purposefully bringing or sending evil to you. Unwisely and incorrectly, they've decided that _you_ are evil when you haven't even done anything to them. Hey, they feel so bad. This attack that has put them in Survival Mode. This couldn't possibly be their fault, so they think--, but it is. They don't believe that the devil exists (maybe they are unsaved) so it must be some natural person's fault. They pick you; they blame or continue to blame you instead of themselves or instead of the devil who is the actual villain.

You know the devil never stops talking, right? So why wouldn't the devil try to keep a wedge between you and former "friends"? Why wouldn't he try to incite a former acquaintance to retaliate against you, even if you haven't done anything that requires retaliation?

Evil is not logical.

Evil is not sane.

It's just evil.

Because the mind is so strong, is one of the WHY's of why God says to keep your mind stayed on HIM. Think on things that are lovely and of good report things that are true, have virtue and if there be any praise. (Philippians 4:8).

The Lord says He will keep your mind in perfect peace.

You will keep *him* in perfect peace,
whose mind *is* stayed *on You,* **because he
trusts you.** *(Isaiah 26:3)*

If your mind is in peace, the body will soon follow. If the mind is dark and evil the body will become dark and evil, sickly, ill.

Trusting God means NOT turning a situation or a problem over and over in your mind. The Bible says don't worry; it says do not be anxious.

My momma always said, *"Give it all to Jesus."*

Saints of God: don't ruminate, meditate, or stay stuck on past hurts, this will enlarge those terrible events, magnify them in your mind.

O magnify the LORD with me, and let us exalt his name together. (Psalm 35:3)

Oh, come let us magnify the LORD together, let us magnify the **Lord** together, --not magnify people, not magnify problems; we are to MAGNIFY the Lord!!!

Trauma

So, don't think on people who are *attached* to those hurts/disappointments, losses, sorrows. Don't spend your time thinking on that, because it will not prosper your mind or your soul, (3John 2). You don't dwell and think on people who are attached to hurts, disappointments, losses, sorrows, and sadness because thinking on them **magnifies** *them*. Thinking about them all day long or intermittently throughout the day you could:

- Blindly curse the people involved while not even intending to, or realizing that you're doing it.

- Blindly IDOLIZE them. That's bound to happen if you're thinking about them all day long. God says to have no idols before Him. Positive or negative, anything you think about more than God is an idol.

- And if you keep thinking on these problems you magnify the wrongs done to you, and stay in unforgiveness, bitterness. You stay in the flesh. There is no blessing in flesh. Walk by the Spirit so you don't fulfill the desires of the Flesh.

- CONJURE up things you want or think you want. Some people call it manifesting – there's a thin line between manifesting something good and conjuring up something evil.

- You'll hurt yourself--, and this is how: As you rehearse wrongs done, your body does not know **when** that happened to you, or *if* it even happened already. Worrying about something that hasn't even happened confuses your mind and body as well. Your body doesn't know if that is currently happening or not. By worrying, you experience the negative event, and in the worst way, because of your powerful mind, at least once before you actually go through it. Maybe you experience it even more than once, depending on how often you worry about it, leading up to the dreaded event.

After the event is over and you **keep** dwelling on it, your mind, your body may think it is *still* happening to you, or that this evil happens every day. The cascade of Survival Mode is a serious downward spiral.

- Continuing in this way, you **traumatize *yourself*.**

- Do not traumatize yourself. The devil loves trauma, physical, emotional, or mental. He can use all kinds of upset. Trauma makes people more controllable, malleable, manipulatable. Don't traumatize *yourself* by dwelling in a place of hurt and evil. Emotional trauma, grief –, the devil uses all that.

- Continuously dwelling on the hurts, wrongs, disappointments, etc. keeps you in your past and reminds you often of your pain and sorrow.

Broken Hearts

The devil especially loves to inflict, and often uses emotional trauma against mankind. It is one of his signature moves. I know that because God is **binding up** broken hearts. Why? Because there are so many broken hearts? Yes, from emotional trauma.

"The Spirit of the Lord GOD *is* upon me; because the LORD hath anointed me to preach good tidings unto the meek; he hath sent me to bind up the brokenhearted, to proclaim liberty to the captives, and the opening of the prison to *them that are* bound; Isaiah 61:1

Why do you think the Lord is _binding up_ broken hearts?

- o To keep them from bleeding? Yes.
- o To keep them from leaking? Yes.
- o To keep them from getting worse? Yes.
- o To keep infection out? Yes.
- o To keep the devil out? Certainly, Yes!

And they should stay that way, until the broken hearts heal.

The devil, if he can, rushes into a broken heart, to a traumatized heart, to someone who is emotionally traumatized. The heart is the source of the fountain that pumps blood to the rest of the body. If the devil can infiltrate or poison the heart, the body's system will get it to the rest of the body. Easy, peasy.

Don't traumatize yourself; dwelling in the doldrums, in the past, in the hurts, and the disappointments. That breaks and keeps the heart broken. Allowing yourself to be soul tied and staying blue, talking, and singing the blues, keeps you soul tied--, and blue. God binds up broken hearts until they are healed, until God can heal it. But you have a part in the healing of your heart – you've got to agree with God so He can do a work in you.

God is carefully guarding your heart whether it is well and whole or whether it is broken, but especially when it is broken. Why? Out of the abundance of the heart the mouth speaks. For out of your mouth flow the issues of life. God binds up that broken heart to keep you from speaking over your life, your whole life, or any part of it with a **broken heart**.

If you narrate your life, prophesy what you will or won't do, what you want to happen or don't want to happen <u>with a broken heart</u>, you've probably said the **opposite** of what God says about you.

Remember, some things cannot happen in the Earth until Heaven, that's God, and Earth—that's you, **AGREE**. So, if you are disagreeing with God can cause:

- Nothing to happen, or
- God will impose His will and something miraculously good will happen, or
- God will relent and give you the broken-hearted prophecy that you for some reason want to endure.

God is binding up broken hearts; He may bind up your broken heart to keep you with your broken heart from speaking over the lives of others. Like so many broken hearted, divorced, or widowed parents, for example, who may speak words that they think are comfort or a blessing to their children, but they really are diminishing, limiting, harmful words. Words like, *Don't trust this one or that one, this type or that type. Those parents are speaking from experience and from their place of hurt, trauma, and loss.* Ideally, you want to minister to your children and others from a place of wholeness, and peace.

Fear, hurt, disappointment, and emotions related to the flesh cause the heart to speak out of that fear, hurt, and disappointment. Unless GOD. Unless

God has bound up that heart and it can't speak right now.

God is guarding, binding your heart to keep the devil out of it. The *infection* that is the devil cannot get in a broken heart that is bound--, what God has shut, no man (or devil) can open (Rev 3:8). Where a wounded heart is cleaned and dressed, and the gauze of God's love and protection is wrapped around it, and it is sealed with the Holy Spirit, no one is getting in there!

If this broken heart is not bound, it will remain broken, fester, or worse sepsis may set in. Sepsis can lead to death. ***Spiritual sepsis*** could lead to spiritual death if it is not treated.

Steps to a victorious life: Renunciation. Repentance. Salvation. Deliverance. Resistance. Live a more godly lifestyle.

More on this in the book, **The Devil Loves Trauma,** by this author.

Messages by these same titles on YouTube, Dr. Miles Channel.

Following After You

And you feel like you've got something or someone **following** you. Well, you've been thinking about the person or persons who did you wrong all day and ½ the night. In this way you are DRAWING that person to you, or possibly keeping them **stuck** to you. This is conjuring up a person; the soul tied do this all the time. One cannot prosper their soul if their soul is soul-tied.

Depending on your faith, for good or evil, you shouldn't be surprised if you keep bumping into people that you're constantly thinking about. Whether you love them or hate them, that's all junk that's still in your trunk; and it's not serving anybody. All that old baggage needs to go; unpack it. Lord, *take this away, I don't need this, I don't want it.*

Or—Maybe you've handled all of your emotional and spiritual baggage from the past, praise God. And you've just now realized that people from your past weren't able to *transition forward,* as you have. People from your past have not moved on; they are still in the past.

Maybe it seems that someone or some ones are *"stalking"* you; they seem to be following your plans, deeds, actions— your failures, maybe. Every time you take off running it feels like they're right behind you. There's something you want to run *toward*, but something heavy seems to be weighing you down, or like a rope wrapped around you, holding you back. Feels like it's making you stand still or worse, dragging you in reverse. You want to run toward your future, your destiny, your career, your education, your marriage and family— children. Seems like there's something weighing you (an evil anchor) Somebody's in your business with their opinion or what not. And maybe it doesn't even scare or bother you anymore.

Don't get used to that.

You really don't want to be bothered by them anymore—you want to tell them, *worry about yourself.* That something holding you down is the junk that you are carrying in your trunk; it is not only *in* your past, but it may also *be* your **past**. All the people who used to know you "when.". You've met God, whether they realize it or not, now they need to get to know you all over again.

No matter what people are thinking about you, no matter what you *think* people are thinking about you, it is what God is thinking about you that is important. It is what you think about yourself that is most important. *Worry about yourself.* Love others as much as it is in you; but worry about yourself. I've adopted an attitude that works for me, maybe it will work for you:

If people want to wait until they get to Glory to find out the Truth about a matter, about you, or about a situation, past or present, that is their option.

Then I let it go. When you can't do no more, you can't do no more. Turn it all over to Jesus and keep it moving.

Trying to press forward, you don't necessarily see what, but something seems to be slowing you down, or stopping every good thing you try to accomplish! It feels like extra weight on you. You're not paranoid. You're just aware. Spiritually awake and alert.

Spiritually Woke

Turning it over to Jesus means prayer, any and all kinds of prayer, especially Warfare Prayer. Once I know it is in the hands of the Lord and He is advocating for me against the enemy of my soul and my very life--, both human and non-human, I can sleep at night. God is and will always be the Victor!

Time has gone by; you've got nothing to do with them. Have had nothing to do with them **for weeks, months, maybe even YEARS.** You two don't have kids or any kind of business or property together. There is nothing tying you together except possibly soul ties, which we will break, in Jesus' Name.

Maybe they don't mean good to you, and you might see them, and they haven't let it go. It's been years. But in your face, they smile.

This is why you have to *discern* every spirit. **If you don't have discernment, you need to ask God for it.** He'll give it to you. I've had to ask Him. He'll show you people right on the spot or maybe He'll show you them in a dream.

I remember a very clear dream about seeing a rat in a garden. The next day I saw a person, that, unfortunately, we were on vacation with at the time, standing three floors up on a balcony. As we were walking back to the hotel, she was standing on the balcony above a garden, observing us. As we approached the balcony where she was standing, I saw a rat in that garden just below her. God let me know she was not to be trusted and it proved very true in upcoming months/years. **She's one of the reasons for this book.**

I've had to let that go.

Goodness and Mercy should be following after you. Sweet perfume, a good smelling aroma, not hurts and evil and disappointments. When you think you're dragging your Ex, you may really *be* dragging your Ex and by so doing he may be dragging you. You can't carry a fully grown human around (in your mind, in your heart and soul) who doesn't want to be carried around, or actually **be** around you. That's a lot of weight to drag. That's when you've tied your soul to a person and trying to stay connected to them—dragging them around.

Whether you want them because they are good or because you can't stop thinking about them because they are bad, either is a soul tie. You should not tie yourself, your soul to a person who means you harm, and/or doesn't want to be tied to you.

Evil, Human Persecutors

Evil. Persecutors. Human persecutors.

For no reason at all. You haven't given him/her/them any reason to hurt you? Harm you? Wish you evil? Pay you back? You don't think so, anyway. You may even know you haven't so, but they persist against you, because *they* can't *get over it*. They are not mature enough. Maybe they are just haters. And that's the definition of a persecutor, when someone is doing something to you that you *don't deserve,* a person who harasses or annoys someone persistently is persecuting them.

Sounds like the devil, doesn't it?

Blessed are the peacemakers, for they will be called sons of God.

Blessed are those who are persecuted because
of righteousness, for theirs is the kingdom of heaven.

Blessed are you when people insult you, persecute you, and falsely say all kinds of evil against you because of me. Matthew 5:9-11

The persecution spoken of in the Bible is for the sake of the Gospel, not just because they hate you. That persecution is for the sake of the Kingdom, because you're saved and profess Jesus and do your ministry calling. The world's persecution is for no reason other than jealousy or evil— they just want to ruin your credibility, your name. They don't want to put any respect on your name. Don't embrace that.

Blessed? It doesn't seem too blessed. You know for sure that it's not you, not you who are carrying junk in your own trunk, it is others trying to force unnecessary burdens and evil load on you. You wish they'd go away, get off your case, stop following your life--, forget you and <u>LOSE</u> your location.

Some or all of them probably need to go away and <u>should</u> go away. They will go away when you **pray** if God doesn't have a purpose in it. If He's not currently teaching you something by it, such as how to rule and reign, how to pray, how to handle iffy, sketchy people and you do ask Him to take it away, I believe He will. When you've learned all the lessons from it, ask God and He will end the persecution.

If you have learned forgiveness, releasing bitterness, if you've released them, I believe when you pray the LORD will take the harassment away. If you've learned everything you can from this already, I believe that the Lord will take it out of your life.

You have got to forgive. Don't hold ought against each other so:

- So, your prayers will be heard,
- So, our offerings will be received by God, and
- So, blessings will come to you.

If there is some junk you need to unpack, let's clear out that trunk. Why are you taking this stuff from place to place? Even though there are also bitter people, people who won't forgive easily, or at all, you do your part, you **forgive them** anyway. Some may have vowed in their heart, *I will never forget or forgive,* or whatever vows they have spoken. That's not you, right? Pray to the Lord that those others you have been involved with will forgive, receive the love of Christ, and walk in His Light instead of making evil vows.

We are going to pray against *human persecutors*. Abel should have prayed this prayer against Cain who persecuted him—to death. David should have prayed this against King Saul who was David's human persecutor; as well against Absalom who also tried to kill David. Naboth should have prayed it against Jezebel, who had him killed. Elijah could have prayed this against the King of Aram and the whole army that came out against him and his armor bearer--, just two people, and God surely rescued Elijah. Joseph needed to have prayed this against 10 of his 11 brothers.

Evil persecutors who are *all up in* your business, on your trail are the ones who won't stop, until you fail or drop, if you don't pray. They are the ones that won't stop until the lessons stop, when you agree with God by **opening your mouth and STOP them.**

Decree & Declare

Hard to believe that these humans are **STILL** in that vortex, still *obsessed* with you. So much time has passed, and they still hold hatred, animosity, and venom against you. You can't just tell some people to *get over it* – it's not that simple if they are not spiritually or emotionally mature yet.

You will have to pray.

It depends on who they are, what they've been through, their temperament, how much God they have on board, and how much soul prosperity they have to forgive wrongs, hurts, or *perceived* wrongs and hurts. In other words, how much spiritual maturity they have, especially since you may not have even done anything to them.

It depends on their emotional maturity. The "stuck" ones could be conjuring evil against you in their hearts. Whether on purpose or by accident, it doesn't matter, they are still blindingly walking in witchcraft and conjuring evil.

And let me add, it depends on how much GOD they have on board to realize who you are to God, who you are in the Spirit, and it might not be a good idea to go against you because they need to know who your GOD is and that when they come up against you, they come up against the Most High God. **He will contend with those who contend with you.**

Contend, LORD, with those who contend with
me;
fight against those who fight against me.
Take up shield and armor;
arise and come to my aid.
Brandish spear and javelin[a]
against those who pursue me.
Say to me,
"I am your salvation."
May those who seek my life
be disgraced and put to shame;
(Psalm 35:1-4)

- The person obsessed with you might not even **KNOW** you. They may be in a relationship with someone that you used to be in a relationship with and blame you as the *cause* of this person's hurt. They are believing whatever tales they've told this new person. They may have told the truth. They may have told the "truth" *as they know it.* They may have gaslighted the new person to get that person to treat them the way they want to be treated.

- They simply believe what this other person said about you. Really, they don't know you.

- They may feel that **<u>you</u>** stole the person they loved/wanted.

- They could be bitter that you took the job they wanted.

- You could be resented for having told the teacher they cheated on the exam because they did. They copied off your paper and got kicked out of school.

You know your own story better than anyone. But God can get you through it and out of it. Are you ready to pray?

Now We Pray

Father, in the Name of Jesus, I come to You repenting of my sins. I repent of every sin, known and unknown where I have sinned against You. Lord, have Mercy on me. I plead the Blood of Jesus.

Lord, have Mercy on those who may have blindly wished evil on me. Touch their hearts so they may know the error of their thinking and their ways. Bind unforgiveness and bitterness from their hearts and let them see You, Lord. Let them seek You and yield to your ways, the ways of understanding, the ways of Peace, the ways of Love.

For those to whom I have offered forgiveness, apologized to, and asked to be forgiven, but they will not forgive, they will not relent of the evil in their heart-- for every unrepentant evil doer, wicked soul, especially those who smile in my face, I come boldly to You in prayer seeking relief. Lord let the powers of the wicked be blown away as the chaff is blown by the wind, in the Name of Jesus.

Let the ways of the wicked powers assigned to any aspect of my life perish, in the Name of Jesus.

Oh Lord, laugh at all evil counselors that are against me; laugh them to scorn. Have them in derision. Break all the evil kings that are gathered against me with a rod of iron.

Father, LORD, dash them to pieces, smite all my enemies on the cheekbone with dirty Holy Ghost slaps.

Oh Lord, break the teeth of the wicked; torment them; make them suffer. Let my enemies fight one another and fall by their own ways, in the Name of Jesus.

Let the wicked be cast out in the multitude of their transgression, in the Name of Jesus.

O Lord, let all my enemies be ashamed and troubled; let them receive sudden shame and take their arrows back. I return to sender every evil arrow.

Arise, O Lord, in Your anger and in Your hot displeasure, because of the rage of my enemies. Oh Lord, let the wickedness of the wicked come to an end.

Lord, prepare the instruments of death against my persecutors.

Return all evil arrows back against my persecutors.

Oh Lord let the enemies of my soul fall into the pit which they dug.

Let the mischief of the oppressors come upon their own heads. Lord, return violence for violence.

Lord, let my enemies fall and perish at Your Holy Presence; contend with those, that contend with me.

Let the net of the enemy catch *his own feet.* Let the wicked be taken in devices that they have imagined, in the Name of Jesus. No weapon formed against me in the heavens, the Earth, the waters, the sun, stars, or moon, in all of the universe shall prosper against me. All creation of GOD obeys the Lord God, and I am a child of the king. I bear the marks of the Lord Jesus in my body.

Elements of Earth, I speak to you; you shall serve me and not harm me, in Jesus' Name.

Lord, break the arm of the wicked. Let the sorrows of the enemies be multiplied. Arise Lord, disappoint the enemy and deliver my soul from the wicked.

Let thunder, hailstones, coals of fire, lightning and arrows from the Lord scatter the forces of the enemy, in the Name of Jesus.

Lord, give me the necks of my enemies.

Let all oppressors be beaten small as the dust before the wind, let them be cast out as the dirt in the streets, in Jesus' Name.

Oh, Lord, swallow the oppressors and persecutors.

Holy Ghost Fire, devour the wicked and their seeds. Deliver my soul from the power of the dog and from the mouth of the lion.

Lord, let the evil devices of the enemy *refuse* to perform. I speak to every evil device, "You will NOT work against me, I am a child of the Only Living God, you will not work against me, in Jesus' Name!"

Let the eaters of flesh and drinkers of blood stumble and fall, in the Name of Jesus.

Lord render to my enemies their just desserts. Let all lips speaking grievous things proudly against me be silenced, in the Name of Jesus.

Lord, send Your Warrior Angels to sow terror and panic in the hearts of all evil doers gathered against me. *Evil shall slay the wicked.* Make them desolate, in the Name of Jesus.

O Lord, fight against them, that fight against me. Let them become confounded and put to shame that seek after my soul, in the Name of Jesus.

Let them be turned back and brought to confusion that devise my hurt, in the Name of Jesus.

Angels of God, chase and persecute the enemies of my soul, in the Name of Jesus.

Let the way of my enemies be dark and slippery, in Jesus's Name.

Lord, do not let my enemies rejoice over me.

Let them be ashamed and brought to confusion together, that rejoice at my hurt, in the Name of Jesus.

Let them be clothed with shame and dishonor, that magnify *themselves* against me, in the Name of Jesus.

Let the sword of the wicked enter into their own heart and let their bows be broken, in the Name of Jesus.

Let all the enemies of the Lord be consumed, in the Name of Jesus.

Oh God, break the teeth of the enemy in their mouth, in Jesus Name.

When the enemy bends his bow to shoot his arrows, let him be cut in pieces, in the Name of Jesus.

Let the wicked fall by the sword and become a portion for foxes, in the Name of Jesus.

Let their table become a snare before them, in the Name of Jesus.

Let that which would have been to their benefit become a trap to them, in the Name of Jesus.

Every evil arrow fired at me or in my direction, return to sender, in Jesus' Name.

Let the extortioner catch all that the enemy has, and let the strangers spoil his labor, in the Name of Jesus.

As he loved cursing, so let it come upon him.

As he delighted not in blessing. So let it be far from him, in the Name of Jesus.

Let them be as grass up on the housetop that withers before it grows up, in the Name of Jesus.

Lord, stretch forth Your hand against my enemies, let the mischief of their own lips cover them, in the Name of Jesus.

Do not grant the desires or devices of the wicked, in the Name of Jesus.

Let burning coals fall upon them in the Name of Jesus.

Add iniquity to their iniquity, in the Name of Jesus.

Let them be covered with reproach and dishonor that seek my hurt, in the Name of Jesus.

Persecute them with tempests, hailstorms, and tsunamis; make them afraid with storms in the Name of Jesus.

My eyes shall see my desire on my enemies.

Give evil and human persecutors that rise up against me memory loss that they forget my name and lose my location, in the Name of Jesus.

Overthrow the violent enemy in Jesus's Name. Lord cast, forth lightning and scatter them.

Let God arise and let all His enemies be scattered, in Jesus's Name.

Let God be exalted above all "*gods*" in the Name of Jesus. Hallelujah.

Father in Heaven, in the Name of Jesus I renounce all evil in my heart, and all evil people who have an evil intent against me whether I list them by name ... one at a time or in an entire group --- LORD, You know.

I ceremoniously separate myself from them, my life from their life/lives, in the Name of Jesus.

I serve him/her/them a bill of divorce. I pull up all hidden documents detailing **EVERY covenant, contract and oath** entangling us and command that they be stamped with the **Blood of Jesus.**

I renounce all evil, all contracts that I have ratified knowingly or unknowingly. I especially renounce covenants and contracts made through physical relations and all curses that go along with sex contracts.

I bind every devil and demon associated with causing those curses to come about and I bind every devil and demon assigned to *carry out* the curse of any evil covenant. I bind them and I cast them out, in the Name of Jesus.

Any part of me that is still loyal to him/her, by the Angels of God, the heavenly host, LORD put those parts to sleep.

I now deed (evil person or entity's) territory in me over to the Kingdom of God—any fragment of their SOUL that I may have, and I request every part of my soul, my being, my life, to be returned to me. I invite you, LORD Jesus to take the Throne and rule over this with your Rod of Iron. Yes, LORD, I pray mercy as I call for judgement on this evil that is against me.

In the Name of Jesus, I now bind all gatekeepers and discover each, and every portal access point belonging to this evil, his/her realm, and his/her inheritance or promised inheritance.

I place the Blood of Jesus upon every portal access point, and I seal every access the with the HOLY Spirit. I declare that they are put to sleep and permanently deactivated from this point in time, forward.

With the Sword of the Spirit, which is the Word of God, I cut myself free from Evil Person's realm, and his/her inheritance in Jesus' Name. I cut myself free from his/her evil cogitations, ruminations, ideas, threats, evil wishes, desires, thoughts, machinations, plans.

I return every form of counterfeit inheritance—any tangible or intangible thing that has tied us together--, jewelry, tokens, letters, books, clothing, gifts of any kind including promised

Wealth, Position, Status, Calling, Ability, Power, Pride, Favors, Seed, and any other form of counterfeit inheritance, in Jesus Name. I refuse it and sever myself from it and from this point in time forward I choose to receive my inheritance in Jesus Christ. Lord, I renounce it. I renounce the covenant /contract made in the Name of Jesus.

I renounce **all** *spirit children* related to this person/relationship/entanglement/association due to **ungodly, unsanctioned, un-covenanted relations**, and by the Blood of Jesus, I undo all quantum entanglements involved in the creation of spirit or synthetic children. I command their judgment and the purging of the realms they occupy by judgment through **Living Water**. I now reclaim every part of me that has been imprisoned by Evil Person, or in realms related to him/her.

In the Name of Jesus, I release forgiveness, by faith to Evil Person for the evil that he/she has done against me, I also discover every part that is a composite of genetic components held together by a cord that binds. I declare that the cords are cut and that each part is separated into its components. I retain **my** parts and surrender the parts that do not belong to me.

Lord, I present my case before you and I seek Your Justice: *As a man sows, so shall he reap.*

Vengeance is yours Father, I command your Heavenly Hosts to bind every part of Evil Person in me and take him/her to where he/she now belongs.

I take authority over every *evil spirit* on the inside of me and around me that has been operating under the authority of Evil Person and declare that you are discovered, apprehended, bound, pierced through, and thrust out of me for judgment. I declare that you are being sent to the abyss for failed assignment.

Lord God, every spiritual object, tattoo, device, label, marker, power source, grid, ley lines, or branding placed in or around every part of me by or because of Evil Person, or by those under his/her authority would be consumed by the Holy Fire of Jesus Christ and totally dissolved.

For the natural children involved: they will not be used, they will not be pawns. They will not be weaponized against either side. They will not be hurt, harmed, or used as monitors from house to house.

Lord, protect the natural children of this relationship, situationship, entanglement, rendezvous, hook up, or whatever it was.

Jesus said, *Suffer the children to come unto Me*. May they meet Jesus, know Jesus, and become saved and children of the Most High God, in Jesus Name, Amen.

In the natural, I pray for peace and if peace is not obtainable, I pray for a *peaceful separation of parties*/entities/people involved and bind their own spirits back to their own bodies, declaring that it shall not rest on me or my house, my household, my life, or future relationships, especially not my children.

Thank You, Lord. Amen.

Thank you for reading, *Lose My Location.*

Other books by this author

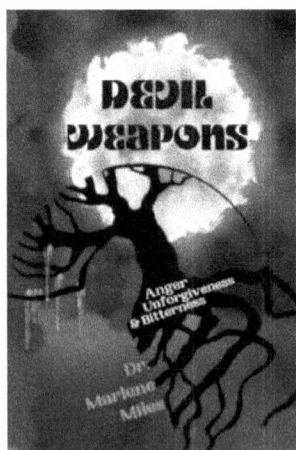

AK: Adventures of the Agape Kid

AMONG SOME THIEVES

As My Soul Prospers

Behave

Blindsided: Has the Old Man Bewitched You?

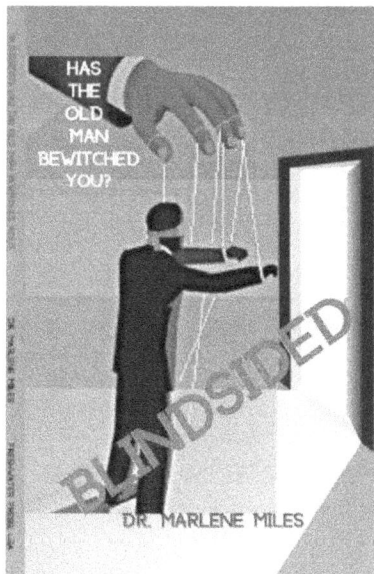

Churchzilla (The Wanna-Be Bride of Christ)

The Coco-So-So Correct Show

Demons Hate Questions

Do Not Orphan Your Seed

Do Not Work for Money

Don't Refuse Me Lord

EVIL TOUCH

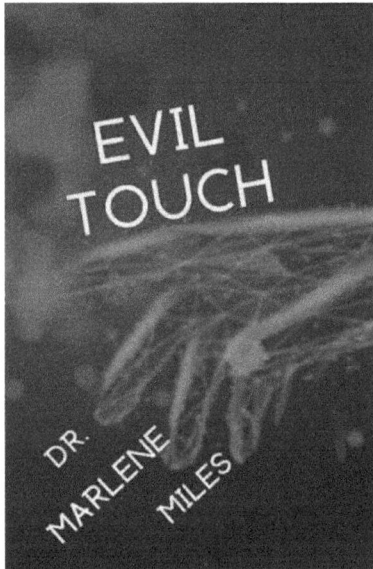

The FAT Demons

got Money?

Let Me Have a Dollar's Worth

Living for the NOW of God

Lord, Help My Debt

Lose My Location

Made Perfect In Love

The Man Safari *(Really, I'm Just Looking)*

Marriage Ed., *Rules of Engagement & Marriage*

The Motherboard: *Key to Soul Prosperity*

My Life As A Slave

Name Your Seed

Plantation Souls

The Poor Attitudes of Money

Power Money: Nine Times the Tithe

The Power of Wealth

Seasons of Grief

Seasons of War

SOULS in Captivity

Soul Prosperity: Your Health & Your Wealth

The *spirit* of Poverty

The Throne of Grace, *Courtroom Prayers*

Warfare Prayer Against Poverty

When the Devourer is Rebuked

The Wilderness Romance

www.ingramcontent.com/pod-product-compliance
Lightning Source LLC
Chambersburg PA
CBHW070547030426

42337CB00016B/2394